TECHNOLOGY IN TIMES PAST

Aztec, Inca and Maya

ROBERT SNEDDEN

An Appleseed Editions book

First published in 2008 by Franklin Watts
338 Euston Road, London NW1 3BH

Franklin Watts is a division of Hachette Children's Books

Franklin Watts Australia
Hachette Children's Books
Level 17/207 Kent St, Sydney, NSW 2000

© 2008 Appleseed Editions

Created by Appleseed Editions Ltd,
Well House, Friars Hill, Guestling,
East Sussex TN35 4ET

Designed by Helen James
Edited by Pip Morgan
Illustrations by Graham Rosewarne
Picture research by Su Alexander

ISBN 978 0 7496 8060 2
Dewey Classification: 609

A CIP catalogue for this book is available from the British Library.

Picture acknowledgements
Page 7t Marco Cristofori/Corbis, b Vanni Archive/Corbis; 8 Guenter Rossenbach/Zefa/
Corbis; 9 Arcaid/Corbis; 10 Massimo Listri/Corbis; 11 Mimmo Jodice/Corbis; 13t Guenter
Rossenbach/Zefa/Corbis, b Bill Ross/Corbis; 14 Bettmann/Corbis; 15 Mimmo Jodice/Corbis;
16 Araldo de Luca/Corbis; 17 Morley von Sternberg/Arcaid/Corbis; 18 Free Agents Ltd/
Corbis; 21t Jose Fuste Raga/Zefa/Corbis, b Sandro Vannini/Corbis; 22 Erich Lessing/AKG
Images; 23 Fine Art Photographic Library/Corbis; 25t Adam Woolfitt/Corbis, b Richard
Cummins/Corbis; 26 Erich Lessing/AKG Images; 27 Richard Hamilton Smith/Corbis; 28 Eye
Ubiquitous/Corbis; 29 Museo Della Civilta Romana Rome/ Gianni Dagli Orti/The Art
Archive; 30 Araldo de Luca/Corbis; 31 Bruce Adams; Eye Ubiquitous/Corbis; 33t Joseph
Martin/AKG Images, b Anders Ryman/Corbis; 34 Araldo de Luca/Corbis; 35 Museo Della
Civilta Romana Rome/Gianni Dagli Orti/The Art Archive; 36 Araldo de Luca/Corbis; 37t
James L. Amos/Corbis, b Macduff Everton/Corbis; 38 Erich Lessing/AKG Images; 39 Owen
Franken/Corbis

Front cover Massimo Listri/Corbis

Printed in China

CONTENTS

THE NEW WORLD

When Spanish explorers first reached the Americas in the 16th century they thought they had discovered a New World. They were surprised to find that this new land was a large continent already occupied by peoples, such as the Aztecs, Inca and Maya, who were part of great civilizations.

MESOAMERICA

The region that includes Mexico and Central America is called Mesoamerica, which means 'Middle America'. Several civilizations had risen and fallen here before Europeans knew it existed. One belonged to the Olmec people, who flourished between 1200 and 400 BC. Another was the mighty Teotihuacan, who were at the height of their power from AD 150 to 450 and who built the largest city in the Americas at the time.

At the start of the 16th century the dominant civilizations of Mesoamerica were the Maya and the Aztecs. The kingdom of the Maya had begun around 1000 BC. It did not have a capital city or a single ruler. Each Mayan city was self-governing, like the city-states of ancient Greece. The Maya were most powerful from around AD 300 to 900. There are still about six million Mayans living in Central America today, mainly in Mexico. Around AD 1200 the Mexica people rose to

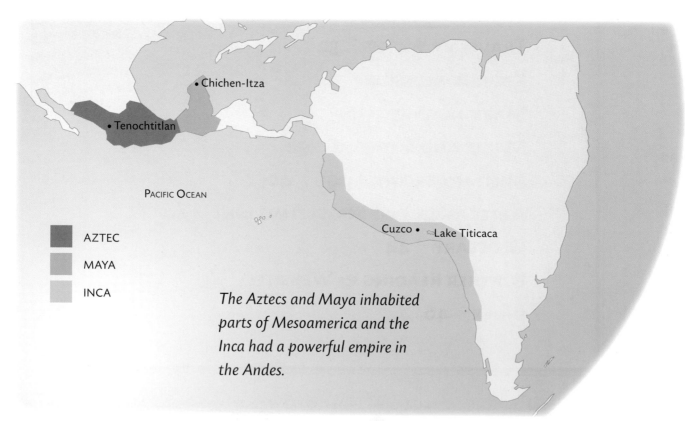

AZTEC

MAYA

INCA

The Aztecs and Maya inhabited parts of Mesoamerica and the Inca had a powerful empire in the Andes.

The Inca city of Machu Picchu attracts many visitors to its remote location in the Andes.

power and built a strong civilization, forging alliances and waging war to extend their control. We know them as the Aztecs.

THE ANDES

The Andes is one of the world's greatest mountain ranges, stretching like a backbone along the length of South America. People have probably lived here for more than 13,000 years. They discovered how to work with gold, silver and copper, and used these metals to make tools and jewellery.

A number of different peoples fought for power in the region, including the Huari, who dominated much of what is now Peru from around AD 500 to 1200. The Huari people

The Maya made many clay figures that were placed beside a body when it was buried.

introduced an agricultural system of terraced fields that helped them to grow more food in the mountains.

In 1438, the Inca people conquered the area around Cuzco, which they made their capital city. They became the dominant civilization in the region, but the Spaniards ended their power a hundred years later.

The civilizations of the Andes and Mesoamerica built magnificent cities, developed their own way of looking at life and created great works of art and learning.

7

BUILDING HOMES

The Aztecs, Inca and Maya built their homes with local materials. Aztec and Maya homes were usually made of mud brick, while the Inca also used stone. The roofs of the houses were thatched with reeds or grasses. Mostly, the houses had just one room with only a little furniture.

Today, Mayan people continue to live in homes built in the traditional style.

AZTEC HOMES

The Aztecs built their homes from adobe, which is a mixture of sun-dried mud and straw, and covered them with a thatched roof. The word 'adobe' is Spanish for 'dried brick'. Aztec homes were open plan, which means they had one big room divided into areas for different activities. There was an inside courtyard with a kitchen area for preparing food, an eating area where the whole family shared a meal, a sleeping area where everyone rested together, and a small family shrine with statues of gods displayed on a table.

INCA HOMES

The Inca people, who lived on the Pacific coast of northwestern South America, also built adobe houses. The roofs were flat and the walls were covered in painted plaster for extra protection.

In mountain towns a typical Inca home was built of stone. In towns, several homes were built together around a central courtyard. Timber beams attached to stone pegs ran across the top of the house, supporting a roof frame that was covered in thatch. Most houses were single storey, although a few had upper floors. If a house had a second storey, it was reached by rope ladders inside the house or by stone steps outside.

The Inca did not spend much time indoors so their homes had little furniture. Many houses had no windows or chimneys, so they must have been very dark and smoky inside.

The doors and windows (if there were any) were not rectangular like ours. Instead, they had two parallel sides and the top of the door or window was narrower than the bottom.

MAYAN HOMES

Many of the Maya who live in rural Mexico today have homes very similar to those built by their ancestors hundreds of years ago.

The walls of Mayan houses are built from woven sticks covered with a mixture of red soil, brush weeds and water, called *embarro*. The roof is made of sloping palm leaves. Mayan houses have a front and back door, but don't have any windows.

People make adobe bricks for their homes in present-day Peru.

CITIES OF THE INCA

The Inca empire stretched from the Pacific coast to the mountains of the Andes. Inca cities were built of local materials. Cuzco, for example, had many stone buildings, such as Sacsayhuaman, while Chan Chan on the coast had mud brick buildings laid out in a grid pattern of straight lines.

The remains of the Inca fortress of Sacsayhuaman stands in Cuzco, Peru.

CAPITAL CITY

The Inca made Cuzco the capital city of their empire. At the time of the Spanish conquest it may have had around 200,000 inhabitants. Legend says that Cuzco was laid out in the shape of a puma, with the fortress of Sacsayhuaman as its head. The closely fitting stone walls of the fortress were 16 metres high. So well did the builders do their work that Cuzco has survived several earthquakes.

INCA MASONS

The Inca were famous for their masonry, or stonework. They cut, ground, and polished blocks of stone until the surface was smooth and perfectly shaped. The workmanship was superb and the stones fitted together so precisely that no mortar was needed to hold them together. Their only tools were stone hammers and wet sand, which they used to polish the blocks.

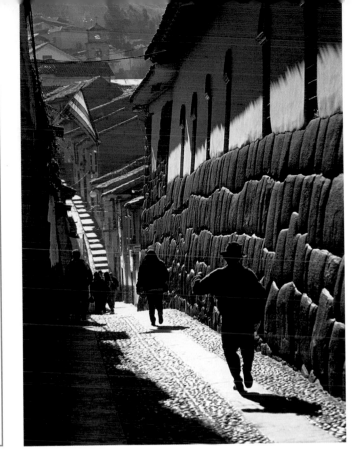

MACHU PICCHU

Around 1450, the Inca built a city called Machu Picchu high in the Andes. The Spaniards never discovered it because it was so remote. It consisted of 143 granite buildings, including many temples and other important buildings. An irrigation system that supplied water fountains may also have carried water into people's homes.

TWO TYPES OF MASONRY

The skilful Inca stonemasons used two types of masonry for their stone buildings – coursed masonry and polygonal masonry.

They used coursed masonry for constructing the walls of important buildings such as palaces and temples. In coursed masonry, all the stones were carefully cut into rectangular shapes and were placed in flat, smooth and horizontal rows. The stones for the higher parts of the wall were smaller than those at the bottom. This made the building look balanced and pleasing to the eye.

The Inca used polygonal masonry to build ordinary people's homes. This involved finding stones of different shapes and carefully fitting them together like the pieces of a jigsaw puzzle. The drystone walls in many parts of the British countryside are examples of polygonal masonry.

The walls in this street (above) in Cuzco, Peru, were once part of an Inca palace.

The stones in this English drystone wall were fitted together with polygonal masonry.

11

CITIES OF MESOAMERICA

The landscape of Mesoamerica ranges from jungle highlands to coastal plains. The Maya built their cities in both highlands and lowlands, whereas the Aztecs built theirs in the highlands. The central areas of Mesoamerican cities were reserved for the palaces of the rulers and for public buildings and temples.

The Avenue of the Dead was the central street in the city of Teotihuacan.

ANCIENT CITY

The city of Teotihuacan is one of the most impressive cities in Mesoamerica. The ruins are about 40 kilometres north-east of present-day Mexico City.

During the 1st and 2nd centuries AD Teotihuacan became the region's largest city, covering around 20 square kilometres and with around 80,000 inhabitants. By the 4th century the city's influence had spread throughout Mesoamerica.

The city was divided in two by the Avenue of the Dead, which is 2.5 kilometres long. Buildings were arranged, often symmetrically, on either side of the avenue. Many buildings in Teotihuacan followed a similar style – with sloping sides and a flat rectangular top.

Later, the Maya adopted this architectural style, known as the *talud-tablero* style. Most inhabitants of the city lived in large apartment blocks that often also housed workshops for making pottery and other crafts.

Who built Teotihuacan remains a mystery. The Aztecs thought it was the Toltecs who were important in the region between the 10th and 12th centuries AD. But we know the city was founded before the Toltec civilization arose. Others think that the Totonac people were responsible, but there is no real evidence to support this claim. Some research suggests that Teotihuacan was a multicultural centre, whose inhabitants came from many regions.

CITY OF CANALS

During the 13th century the Aztecs arrived in the Valley of Mexico, led by their chief, Tenoch. They were a nomadic people who, according to their legends, had come from a place called Aztlan in the north of Mexico. Finding the best land in the valley already occupied by rival peoples, they settled on two small swampy islands in Lake Texcoco. From a small settlement of reed and grass huts, the city of Tenochtitlan began to grow.

The Aztecs developed the *chinampa* system of farming that allowed them to reclaim land from the swamps (see page 16) and to make it fertile and productive. People travelled along the city's many canals, while causeways linked the city to the mainland and allowed smaller communities to grow. By 1519, there were around 400,000 people living in and around Tenochtitlan, making it the largest population centre in Mesoamerica. Today, Mexico City stands on the site of Tenochtitlan.

THE BALLGAME

A sport called the ballgame was played throughout Mesoamerica. The aim was to put a rubber ball through stone rings at the opponents' end of the court. Every city had a ballcourt. The largest, at Chichen Itza, was 185 metres long and 68 metres wide. The Maya saw the game as a battle between the people of Earth and the forces of the underworld, while the Aztecs saw it as a fight between the moon and the sun. The game was violent and sometimes a player died.

The remains of a Mayan ballgame court has been found at Uxmal in Mexico.

THE PYRAMIDS OF MESOAMERICA

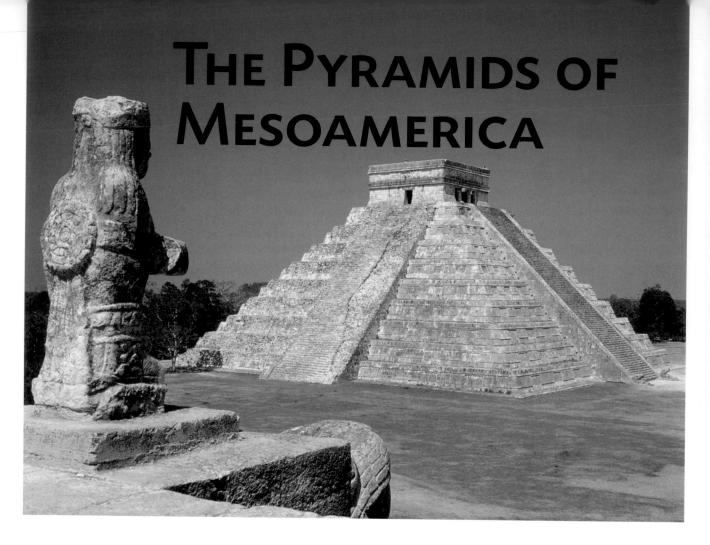

The Aztec and Maya built pyramids in their cities in Mesoamerica. Apart from the Egyptians no other civilization has built such structures on a large scale. The Egyptians built pyramids as tombs for their rulers, but the Mesoamerican pyramids were temples to the gods.

The temple pyramid of Kukulkan stands at Chichen Itza in Mexico.

STEPPED PYRAMIDS

Unlike smooth-sided Egyptian pyramids, Mesoamerican pyramids usually had steps on one or more sides leading up to a temple on the top. Some pyramids were so steep that the top couldn't be seen from ground level.

The Maya often built astronomical observatories as well as temples at the top of their pyramids. The temple pyramid of Kukulkan in the Mayan city of Chichen Itza

was built so that priests could study the stars in the heavens. It has four staircases of 91 steps, one on each side. Together with the platform on the top this makes 365, the number of days in a year.

On the days of the spring and autumn equinoxes (when the days and nights are the same length) the main stairway of the pyramid casts a shadow that looks like the body of a serpent. As the sun moves across the sky the shadow moves down the pyramid to link up with a huge serpent's head carved in stone at the foot of the steps. The Maya believe this represents the god Quetzalcoatl, the Feathered Serpent, who was important throughout Mesoamerica as a god of creation and a giver of life.

THE CHIRPING PYRAMID

The temple pyramid of Kukulkan is remarkable in another way. If you stand at the foot of the pyramid and clap your hands together the echo that comes back sounds remarkably like the chirp of the quetzal, a bird that is sacred to the Maya. Many archaeologists believe that the Maya designed the pyramid to produce this acoustic effect.

THE GREAT PYRAMID

The Great Pyramid of Cholula in Mexico is considered to be the largest monument in the world. It was built as a temple to the god

MOVING BLOCKS

The Maya, the Aztecs and the Inca had no wheeled vehicles or pulleys. How they managed to move the enormous blocks of stone they used for building remains a mystery. We also have little idea how they raised the blocks into position. Perhaps they built ramps as the Egyptians did: once hundreds of men had dragged the stones up and put them into position, the ramps were removed.

Quetzalcoatl and has been added to by many generations of many peoples, from the 2nd century BC up until the early 16th century AD. Archaeologists have discovered more than eight kilometres of tunnels inside.

A carving of the feathered head of the god Quetzalcoatl has been found at the city of Teotihuacan.

15

FARMING

Farming was very important to the thriving populations of the Aztec and Inca empires. The people of the Andes and Mesoamerica had a simple but nutritious diet, and maize and different varieties of beans were important crops. The Aztec and Maya grew tomatoes and avocados, while the Inca had many kinds of potato.

Aztec farmers had no ploughs or work animals such as oxen and horses, so they relied on their own muscle power. The Incas had llamas, but these animals were not strong enough to carry heavy loads.

CANALS AND MOUNDS

Often, the land was poor or difficult to work, so farmers invented ways to get the most from the soil. The Aztecs developed a unique system of farming where they reclaimed land from swamps and shallow lakes by making *chinampas*. The farmers, or *chinamperos*, dug out canals in the swamp, piling up the scooped-out earth on top of the reeds. In this way they formed mounds, or *chinampas*, that were bordered on at least three sides by canals. Here, the farmers grew their crops.

Each *chinampa* was a few metres across and around 30 to 40 metres long. Posts, or woven vines and branches, stabilized the sides of each *chinampa*. Often, willow trees were planted along the edges to help prevent erosion of the soil. The willows were also used for firewood and for building.

Workers tend a chinampa *in Xochimilco at the southern end of Mexico City.*

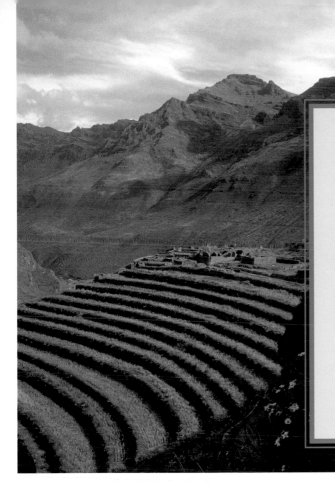

CREATING TERRACES

Farming on the side of a mountain is hard, as rainwater washes the soil away. The Inca solved this problem by building terraces. They created a number of giant steps up the side of a hill or mountain, and hauled up soil in baskets from the plains below. All their hard work was rewarded by the increased yield in the crops that were grown on the terraces. Inca terraces were so successful that they are still used in the Andes today.

Crops are grown on terraces in mountain farms in a highland valley in the Andes.

Maize was a very important crop for the people of Mesoamerica and the Andes.

The *chinampa* system of agriculture was so successful that the Aztecs often had a surplus of food. This helped the growth of the Aztec culture as many people were freed from the job of growing food and so turned to crafts and other studies.

GROWING SEEDS

The *chinamperos* started growing their plants in nurseries, which were located at one end of the *chinampa* beside a canal. They spread a thick layer of mud over a bed of waterweeds and then cut the land into blocks called *chapines* when it had set.

The *chinampero* made a hole in each *chapine*, dropped in a seed, then covered it with manure. The seeds were protected from frost by reeds and kept well watered. When it was ready the seedling was transplanted, still in its *chapine*, to a place on the *chinampa*, then covered with canal mud.

FOOD PREPARATION

The peoples of Mesoamerica and the Andes ate a variety of meat and fish. They hunted animals such as wild pigs and deer with bows and arrows, and with clubs. In both regions fishermen used harpoons, nets and fishhooks made of bone or thorns to catch sea creatures.

POTATO VARIETIES

The potato plant is a native species of the Andes, which means it grows there naturally. Potatoes became a staple part of the Inca diet. The Inca grew around 200 different varieties of potato. A food that we take for granted today was unknown outside South America before the Spaniards brought potatoes back to Europe.

FREEZE DRYING

The Inca developed very efficient ways of preserving, transporting and storing food. They built and maintained food storehouses throughout the empire to supply the army wherever it went.

The Inca found a way of freeze drying food. They left potatoes out at night to freeze in the low temperatures at high altitudes. During the day, when the temperature of the air rose, they trampled the potatoes under their feet, squeezing out the water, which then evaporated.

After a few days, they ended up with a dried potato product, known as *chuño*, which could be kept for over a year if stored carefully. It was used to make *chuño* flour or added to soups and stews. The Inca used a similar process to freeze dry meat to make *charqui*. Today, we make a dried beef snack called jerky, which gets its name from *charqui*.

A street vendor sells different varieties of potato at a market in Pisac, Peru.

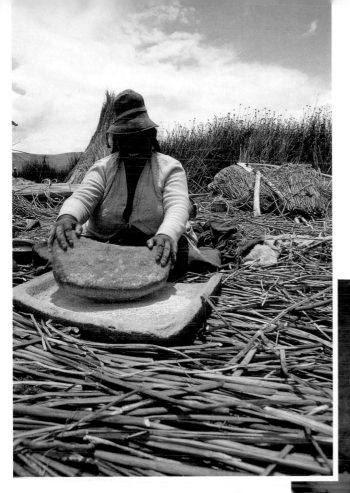

A woman grinds maize with a large stone while she sits on the rushes of a floating island at Lake Titicaca, Peru.

Purepecha women in Mexico prepare tortillas *and bake them over fires.*

MOTHER MAIZE

The main cereal crop in both the Andes and Mesoamerica was maize. Maize is a particularly nutritious plant that grew well there and provided plenty of calories. It was so important to the people of the region that the Maya called it *kana*, which means 'our mother'.

TORTILLAS AND TAMALES

A common way of preparing maize was to mash it with a round grinding stone (called a *mano*) against a flat stone (called a *metate*) to make corn meal. This was mixed with water to make a dough for making *tortillas*, a type of pancake that was a staple part of the Aztec diet. The *tortillas* were cooked over a fire on a pottery disc called a *comal*. Both the Aztecs and Inca ate *tamales*, a sort of steamed maize parcel stuffed with vegetables and meat.

A VERSATILE PLANT

Another source of food for the Aztecs was the *maguey* plant, which is also known as the agave. It was a versatile plant because it had many uses. The Aztecs brewed the sap into a beer-like drink called *pulque*. They turned the thorns into needles and used the plant's fibre to weave rope.

TEXTILES AND CLOTHING

The peoples of Mesoamerica and South America were skilled weavers who made textiles from plant fibres – mainly cotton, but also with fibres from yucca and agave plants. In the Andes the Inca wove cloth from the wool of animals such as the alpaca, vicuña and llama, as well as from cotton.

SPINNING AND DYEING

The Inca spun fibres into yarn using a technique that has been used by people around the world. A weighted stick, called a hand spindle, was set spinning and the spinner teased out the fibres, winding them around the spindle as it turned to form the thread.

The yarn was dyed before it was woven into cloth. The Inca made dyes from a variety of plants and other natural sources. Grinding up cochineal beetles, which are found on cactus plants, made a red dye, for example. It took about 70,000 beetles to make half a kilogram of dye. The Inca made a purple dye from a shellfish found on the Pacific coast. This was similar to the imperial purple dye that was used by the emperors of ancient Rome.

THE BACKSTRAP LOOM

The most common type of loom was the backstrap loom. People throughout the Americas used this simple but very effective piece of technology. The backstrap loom has two wooden poles called loom bars that hold the vertical warp threads. One bar is hung by a cord on a convenient tree or post.

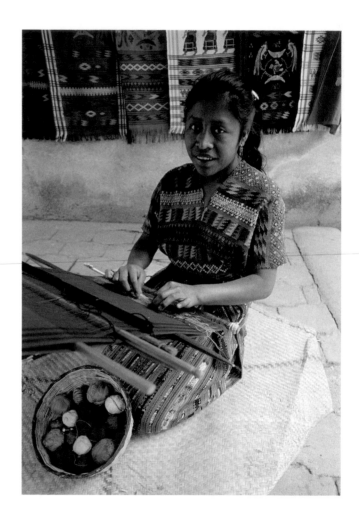

A Maya woman from Guatemala weaves cloth using a backstrap loom.

An adjustable strap worn around the weaver's waist fixes the other loom bar. The weaver keeps the yarn taut by leaning backwards against the strap.

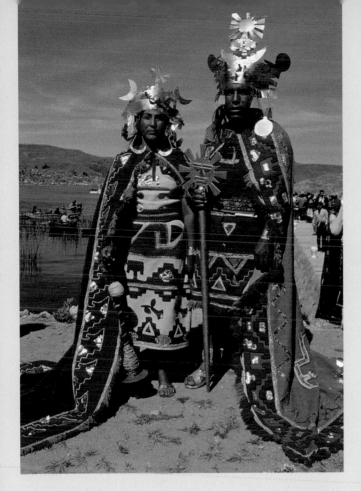

Peruvians in traditional costume celebrate the festival of the First Inca, who landed on the shores of Lake Titicaca after descending from the sun.

Inca men wore a loincloth, sleeveless tunic and cloak, while women wore sleeveless dresses secured with waist sashes.

Aztecs and Inca of high status wore colourful, decorated clothes of the finest materials. The clothes of high-ranking Inca had geometric designs called *tocapus* woven into the cloth across the waistband.

What people wore

The kind of clothes a person wore indicated his or her place, or status, in society. An ordinary Aztec man wore a loincloth and a cape that stopped above his knee. If he wore a cape that reached his ankles he was committing an offence that was punishable by death! Aztec women wore skirts and tunics which they wrapped around themselves.

FEATHERWORKING

Featherworkers were some of the most skilled Aztec craftsmen. They made elaborate headdresses for warriors, priests and other important people. The feathers were fixed individually to a reed framework by tying them with thread and were often trimmed with precious stones, gold and silver.

A drummer wears a traditional Aztec headdress with red and blue feathers.

21

Ceramics

The people of the Andes and Mesoamerica did not use a potter's wheel or a kiln. They made ceramics by shaping coils of clay by hand, by moulding the clay and by carving. Much of their pottery was plain and simple and intended for everyday use. They also made beautiful decorated ceramic pieces for religious ceremonies and for the wealthier members of society.

Aztec bowls decorated with images of skulls.

Slipware

The people of Mesoamerica often produced a type of pottery called slipware. Pottery pieces were treated with a semi-liquid clay, called slip, before they were fired. Different coloured slips were used to paint decorations on the pots. Glazes were very rarely used on the pottery.

One of their decorative techniques involved covering the shaped pot with wax or gum, which was then partly scraped away to leave a pattern. Next, the whole pot was covered in a pigment. When the pot was fired the gum burned away, leaving only the areas that had been scraped free of gum with colour.

Open firing

The potters of the Americas did not use kilns to fire their pottery, as people did elsewhere in the world. Instead, they fired their pieces of pottery in an open fire or placed them in a pit in the ground over which a fire was built. Although they had no kilns the potters still managed to create a type of pottery known as blackware. Usually, this is done by closing the kiln to prevent oxygen from reaching the pots during the firing process. The iron in the clay combines with other chemicals, turning the pot black or dark grey.

22

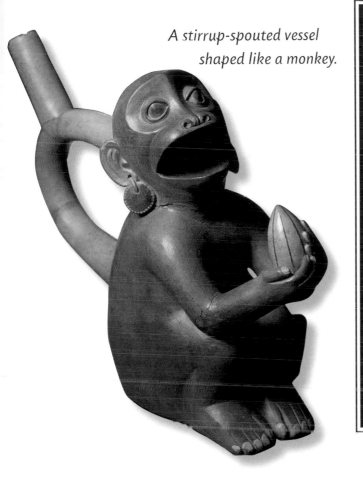

A stirrup-spouted vessel shaped like a monkey.

SOUTH AMERICAN POTTERY

The centres of pottery in South America were in present-day Bolivia and Peru. The Moche people in northern Peru made many pots that had stirrup spouts and depicted all kinds of themes.

The Inca usually produced their pottery to standard shapes, often using moulds. One of the most typical of these designs is the *aryballos* jar. This had a conical base, so presumably it had to be placed in some sort of stand. It also had two handles set low on the body and a flaring neck. Most Inca pottery was polished red, with geometric patterns in red, white or black.

This Mayan bowl is decorated with the heads of three quetzal birds.

23

METALWORKING

Precious metals, such as gold, silver and platinum, were worked 3,500 years ago in Peru. By the 16th century, the peoples of Mesoamerica and the Andes had developed a range of metalworking skills – mainly using gold, silver and copper, but also tin, lead and platinum. They did not work with iron.

MINING AND PANNING

Metals came from mines with narrow tunnels as deep as 40 metres, which followed a rich vein of metal. Metals were also washed from river gravel by panning: digging sticks hardened by firing were used to break up the river bottom and the loosened material was sifted in shallow trays. Sometimes the sifting revealed flecks of precious metals that had been washed down from the mountains.

NATIVE COPPER

Copper is one of the few metals that is found on its own – that is, not combined with another element. This is called native copper and it does not need to be smelted to separate it from other compounds. It was used to make jewellery and tools for ordinary people.

This ornamental jaguar is made from native copper.

GOING FOR GOLD

Goldsmiths had a way of treating *tumbaga* to increase the amount of gold on the surface of the alloy (and so improve its appearance). They rubbed it with the juice of a plant, probably a type of wood sorrel. The juice contains oxalic acid, which dissolves the copper but leaves the gold untouched.

Native copper was also combined with gold to make *tumbaga*, an alloy that is harder than pure gold. The ratio of gold to copper varied widely. Some *tumbaga* was almost entirely gold, while some was almost entirely copper.

COLD WORKING

South American metalworkers were good at working with gold when it was cold. This is called cold working. They could also produce a vessel from a flat sheet of gold – a technique known as raising – and press the gold over moulds to make a series of identical pieces.

The earliest known goldwork is almost 3,000 years old. It consists of embossed sheet gold decorations and was discovered in Chongoyape, Peru. Embossing is a method of decorating metals: hammering and punching the back of the piece produces raised patterns on the surface of the metal.

Andean people pan for gold today using similar techniques to their ancestors.

Metalworkers in Ecuador made fine and elaborate beads from an alloy of gold and platinum. They did this by sintering, which is a technique that involves welding together small particles of metal by alternately hammering and heating – but without melting the metals. The Ecuadoreans used gold dust and small grains of platinum obtained from rivers.

CASTING METAL

The Moche people who lived in northern Peru from about 200 BC to AD 600 were skilled metalworkers. They may have been the first to cast metal around AD 100. This involves pouring molten metal into a mould to produce a shape. The technique probably spread northwards and reached the civilizations of Mesoamerica in about AD 900.

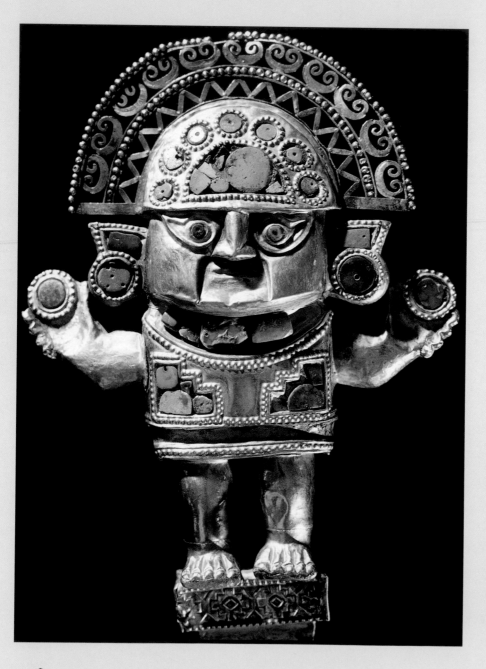

WIND OVENS

The Inca smelted metals in clay furnaces that burned charcoal. They made holes in the front of the furnaces so the wind increased the heat of the fire to make it hot enough to melt the metals. They placed these wind ovens, or *huaira*, on a windy hillside.

GOLD-PLATING

The Moche developed a way of gold plating copper. They dissolved gold in a strong acid and placed a copper object in the liquid. The gold coated the object, which was removed and then heated to bind the gold permanently to the copper.

A gold ornament which the Aztecs wore on their lips.

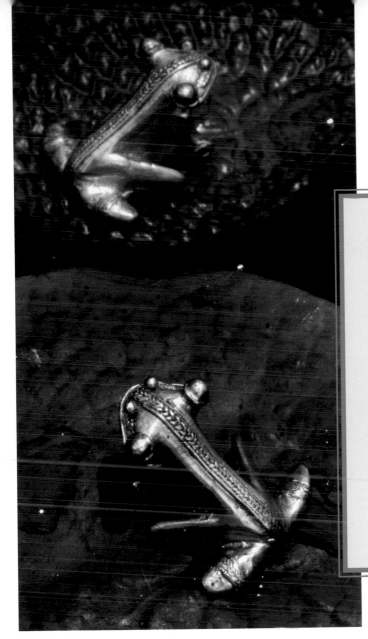

These ornamental frogs from Panama have been cast in gold.

SWEAT OF THE SUN, TEARS OF THE MOON

Gold and silver had great significance for the Inca people. They called gold 'the sweat of the sun' and silver 'the tears of the moon'. Their gold and silver objects were mostly for religious ceremonies and as jewellery for the rich and powerful. The Inca didn't need money. The people worked for the empire building roads and farming crops, for example, and in turn the empire supplied them with clothing and food.

AZTEC GOLD

Goldsmiths were among the most important men in Aztec society. The secrets of their craft were passed from father to son. They made intricate objects using the lost wax method of casting.

This method involved making a wax model of an object and covering it with clay. The clay was fired to harden it and the melted wax was removed, leaving a hollow mould that was shaped like the model. The goldsmith then poured molten gold into the mould. Once the metal had hardened, the mould was broken to reveal the object.

The lost wax method of casting metal objects became a highly developed craft in Mesoamerica and elsewhere. Goldsmiths of the Mixtec people, who were conquered by the Aztecs 30 years before the Spanish arrived, produced gold objects that were very precise and realistic. In the region now known as Panama, craftsmen made tiny gold frogs of such delicacy that they must be viewed under a magnifying glass to appreciate them fully.

Objects of gold and silver were cast by a two-stage process: the gold part was cast first and the silver, which has a lower melting point, was then cast on to the gold.

PRECIOUS STONES

The craftsmen of the Andes and Mesoamerica made many beautiful objects using precious stones. The Inca greatly valued the blue-green turquoise, which they worked into objects of gold and silver. The Mesoamericans favoured jade – its green colour was associated with water and maize, both of which were essential to life.

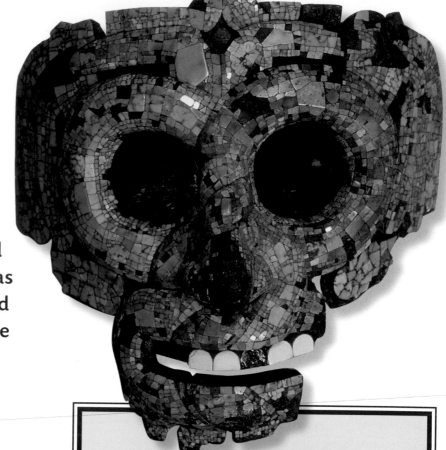

A STONE-AGE CULTURE

The Mesoamerican civilizations were stone-age cultures. Metals were little used for practical purposes by people such as the Aztecs. Although they did have some copper tools, metals such as gold were mostly used for decoration.

Most of the tools used in Mesoamerica were made from stone, such as the glassy volcanic rock called obsidian that they used to make blades. Obsidian blades were used for everything from the ritual killing of sacrificial victims to the preparation of food in the home. The skills of the Aztecs in working and carving stones was second to none.

MAKING MOSAICS
Turquoise, a rare and valuable blue-green mineral, was popular with the Aztecs as well as the Inca. They would grind and polish turquoise to make thin, irregular plates which they used in mosaics on pendants, masks and other decorated items. The mosaic pieces were fixed in place with a variety of glues, such as tree resins and the sap of particular orchids.

Mesoamericans made this turquoise mask (above) to represent the god Quetzalcoatl.

A modern stoneworker preparing gemstones.

This Mayan pendant (below) was carved from jade.

SHAPING STONES

The stoneworkers of the Americas shaped hard stones, such as jade, quartz, amethyst and turquoise, by grinding with abrasives. The abrasives were quartz or jade that had been crushed and pulverized into different-sized granules – from roughly the size of salt grains to the finest polishing powder, which was as smooth as flour.

The gemstone workers were called lapidaries. They began their work with the coarsest grit for the initial carving and shaping of the stone. As the piece took shape, they used finer and finer abrasives. Eventually, they gave the stone a final, mirror-like polish by applying the polishing powder with a piece of wet cloth or leather.

CUTTING AND DRILLING

Tools for cutting pieces of jade and other hard stones were varied. Stoneworkers used a thin slab of sandstone or an abrasive grit glued (perhaps with rubber) to a piece of wood. Another tool was made from wet strips of leather coated with an abrasive powder which were pulled back and forth in a sawing motion across the stone.

Rotary drills, made from reeds or bone, and spun by twirling them between the palms of the craftsman's hands, were also used with grit. The stoneworkers had to drill holes to make beads and pendants, but it must have been extremely slow and hard work.

INCA ROADS

The Inca did not invent the wheel (and neither did the Aztecs), but they built a remarkable system of roads linking the various parts of their empire. Two main roads ran from north to south, one following the coast and the other following the line of the Andes.

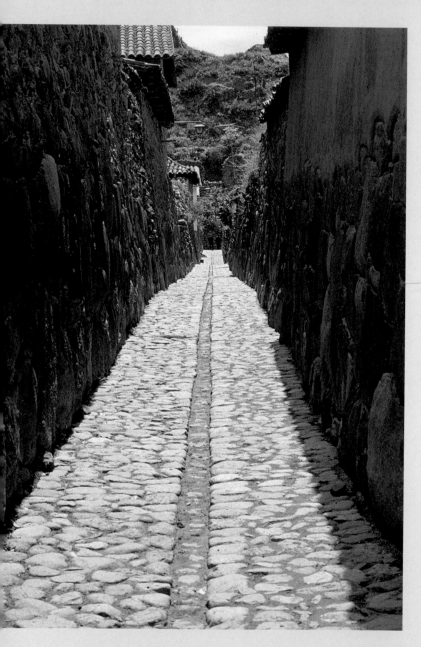

A cobbled alley in Pisac, Peru, starts the Inca Trail to Machu Picchu.

COMMUNICATIONS NETWORK

The roads were the empire's communications network. Ordinary people weren't allowed to use them at all. Messengers, called *chasquis*, ran along the roads carrying messages to and from the capital. They worked like relay runners, one man taking over from another at stone shelters placed along the way. In one day a chain of runners could carry a message 240 kilometres.

Larger resthouses called *tambos* were built beside the roads. These were equipped with food and military supplies for the soldiers of the Inca army who also used the roads.

TWO MAIN ROADS

The most important road was the Andes route, called the Camino Real in Spanish, which ran for over 5,000 kilometres. It began in Quito, Ecuador, passed through the capital city Cuzco, and ended in what is now Tucumán, Argentina. At its highest the Camino Real reached altitudes of over 5,000 metres. The coastal road, El Camino de la Costa, ran parallel to the sea for about 4,000 kilometres and was linked to the Camino Real by many smaller side roads.

THE LAST BRIDGE

The greatest Inca rope bridge crossed the Apurimac Canyon on the Camino Real, a road in the Andes to the north of Cuzco, Peru. The canyon was 67 metres wide and the bridge was 36 metres high. The last remaining Inca bridge still spans the Apurimac River today. Every year around a thousand local men get together to rebuild it, using the same techniques that the Incas used.

The Inca constructed rope bridges so they could cross rivers and canyons.

The coast road was up to five metres wide and lined with mud walls where it passed through irrigated valleys. Fruit trees were planted to give shade. The mountain road was narrower and unwalled. It zigzagged up slopes and stone steps were cut where it was very steep. Wide causeways paved with flat stones were built where the road crossed marshy ground.

ROPE BRIDGES

Where the roads crossed canyons in the mountains the Inca built rope suspension bridges that were strong enough for pack animals and travellers on foot.

To make a rope bridge the Inca placed a pair of heavy stone anchors on either side of the canyon and linked them with strong cables of woven *ichu* grass, which grows widely in the Andes and was also used to thatch roofs. Branches were plaited between these cables to form the walking surface of the bridge. Two more cables were put in place as guard rails. The bridges were so heavy that they tended to sag in the middle and they swayed in high winds. Local villagers were responsible for the upkeep of the bridges and the cables were replaced annually.

TRAVEL BY WATER

The Inca lived by lakes and rivers in the Andes mountains and by the coast of the Pacific Ocean, taking their fishing boats out to cast their nets, and perhaps to trade far afield. The Aztecs built their capital city on a lake, so they naturally made boats to travel around in.

REED BOATS

In many areas timber was in short supply so the Inca used a type of reed called *totora* that grew around the lakes. They cut and trimmed the reeds and bound them in tight bundles that were light, strong and buoyant.

A number of bundles were tied together to form each boat. They were flexible and could be curved to form the pointed bow of the boat, allowing it to slip through the water. People living by Lake Titicaca in Peru still make these reed boats, called *balsas*, today.

Thor Heyerdahl's balsa raft Kon-Tiki *is on display in Oslo, Norway.*

CANALS AND CANOES

Both the Maya and the Aztecs made canoes from hollowed-out tree trunks for travelling along the many waterways in the Valley of Mexico. The Aztec capital of Tenochtitlan was crisscrossed by canals that served as its main thoroughfares. They were often crowded with canoes carrying produce to and from market. The Aztecs had no wheeled vehicles so canoes were the most efficient way of bringing goods into the city. Many homes backed on to one of the canals and many probably had a canoe tied up outside.

DID THE INCA CROSS THE PACIFIC?

In 1947 the Norwegian explorer Thor Heyerdahl set out to prove his theory that people from South America had settled islands in the South Pacific. In Peru, his team built a raft using balsa wood logs and other materials, such as bamboo and banana

A mother and her child (left) sit in their reed boat on Lake Titicaca in the Andes.

leaves, in traditional Inca style. He called it *Kon-Tiki*, after an old name for the Inca sun god. Heyerdahl and his crew sailed across the Pacific for 101 days, covering nearly 7,000 kilometres before running aground in the Tuamotu Islands. Although Heyerdahl's theory was never proved, evidence has emerged recently that trade did take place between South America and islands in the South Pacific before the Spanish arrived.

BOWMEN IN CANOES

Canoes played a part in the defence of Tenochtitlan against the Spaniards. The Spaniards tried to enter the city along one of the causeways that joined the city to the mainland. Aztec bowmen moved swiftly along the canals in their canoes, coming at the Spaniards from both sides of the causeway and firing arrows at them.

KEEPING RECORDS

We see words all the time – in books, magazines and newspapers and on signs, computer screens and mobile phones. Imagine trying to run a civilization without a written language. The Inca kept no written records, while the Aztecs and Maya had a complex picture writing system.

KNOTTED STRINGS

The Inca recorded information on devices called *quipu*. Basically, a quipu was a cord from which a number of knotted strings, made from alpaca or llama wool or cotton were hung. The arrangement and sizes of the knots tied on these strings held the information. Some *quipus* have been discovered with more than 2,000 strings, so the information they carried was probably quite complex.

So far as we know, *quipus* were used to keep records of things bought and sold, tax records, population numbers and anything else that could be counted. They were also used in a similar way to calendars to record and keep track of special events.

Some researchers believe that *quipu* knots may be a system of writing. Some sequences of knots appear to form a code, standing for a place or a person, rather than just a number. The position of different strings and their colour might also play a part in the code. Nobody knows for certain.

These knotted strings are a quipu *that was made in Peru between 1430 and 1532.*

The Codex Cospi is a kind of calendar that contained information to help the Aztecs predict the future.

TALKING PICTURES

The people of Mesoamerica had a picture writing system, similar to the hieroglyphs of ancient Egypt. The Maya's system was the most fully developed and was composed of many detailed pictures called glyphs. Each glyph stood for a word or a part of a word.

A glyph can be both an idea and a sound. A number was shown as a number or as the god associated with that number.

The Aztecs had a picture language, too, although most Aztecs were illiterate. War was shown by a picture of a shield and a club. Talking was a little scroll coming from someone's mouth. They also had pictures for descriptive names – Chimalpopoca, for example, means 'smoking shield'. The symbols in an Aztec manuscript are not placed one after the other like words in a book. They are like an artistic composition where many things may be going on. Every symbol gives a clue to the reader who has to decipher what is happening.

The glyphs in a Mayan codex are very difficult to decipher.

THE MAYA CODICES

The Maya codices (singular codex) are books written in glyphs on long strips of paper, several metres in length, made from the inner bark of the fig tree. Only four of these codices survive today. Much of what we know about the Maya, such as their knowledge of astronomy, has been learned from the codices.

MARKING TIME

Societies have always needed a way to mark time. The Egyptians needed to know when the Nile flooded so they could prepare their fields in time. The Maya believed that it was very important to perform ceremonies on the correct day. We may want to remember a friend's birthday. For all these things you need a calendar.

THE MAYAN CALENDAR

The Mayan calendar is very complex, but very accurate. It uses three different systems for calculating dates: the Haab (the civil calendar), the Tzolkin (the divine calendar) and the Long Count. It was adopted by other peoples of Mesoamerica, including the Aztecs, who didn't make changes but replaced the Mayan names for the days and months with their own.

The Haab is divided into 18 months of 20 days each and five extra days, making 365 days in total. The days of the month were

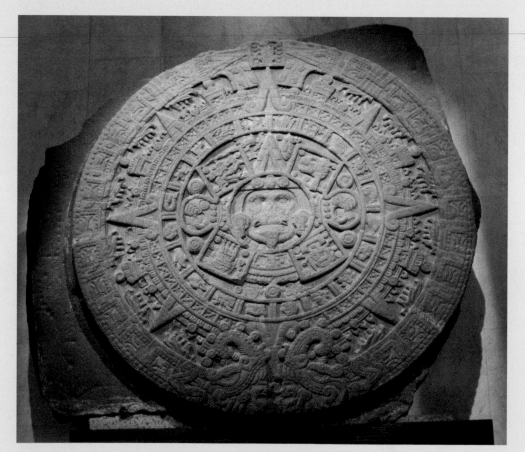

This circular sculpture is thought to be an Aztec calendar stone.

numbered from 0 to 19 – the Maya were unique in having a 'zero' day. They also knew that a year was 365 and a quarter days long.

THE LONG COUNT

The Long Count was based on a 360-day *tun* (a measure of time, like a year) and a number system based on 20. Four hundred *tuns* made a *baktun* of 144,000 days, and 13 *baktuns* equalled a Great Cycle of 5,130 years. The Maya, Aztecs and other Mesoamerican peoples believed that at the end of each Great Cycle the world ceases to exist and a new one is created. If you'd like to note it in your diary, the current Great Cycle ends on 23 December 2012.

The Maya had two different week lengths: a numbered week of 13 days, and a named week of 20 days. These weeks ran together in a cycle that repeated every 260 days. This was the Tzolkin calendar. Each day had different associations of good and bad luck.

THE CALENDAR ROUND

Together, the Tzolkin and the Haab systems formed a cycle that repeated once every 52 years. This was the Calendar Round. The peoples of Mesoamerica looked on the end of each cycle with trepidation.

The Aztecs celebrated it as the Binding Up of the Years, or the New Fire Ceremony. All fires were allowed to burn out on the last day of the cycle. Then, as the first day of the new cycle began, Aztec priests lit a new sacred fire on the breast of a sacrificial victim. From the flames of this fire the people relit their own fires and began feasting.

MAGIC AND MEDICINE

The peoples of Mesoamerica and the Andes believed
that illness was caused by evil magic or punishment by
the gods. Any cure therefore had to be a magical one
or brought about by pleasing the god in question. But
they also observed which of the magical cures worked
and built up a knowledge of medicinal plants.

La Medicina Herbolaria. (Códice Badiano).

HERBAL MEDICINE

The Inca often treated people's illnesses and
ailments with a variety of herbal remedies,
such as the leaves of the tobacco and coca
plants. For example, inhaling tobacco powder
was thought to clear the head. The leaves of
the coca plant were used for relieving pain,
increasing alertness and boosting endurance.
The Aztecs grew plants for medicinal use in
special gardens. Medicinal seeds and roots
were often combined with vanilla or cocoa
to make them taste better.

An Inca skull showing evidence of trepanation.

Aztec medical procedures (left), such as treating a fever, were recorded in the Codex Badianus.

EARLY SURGERY

The Aztecs and Inca had a good knowledge of the way the body worked and could treat wounds and broken limbs. They had few medical instruments. Their knives were made of flint or obsidian stone and they stitched wounds using human hair or vegetable fibres with needles made of human or animal bone.

The treatment for a broken limb was first to press the area of the fracture, stretch the bone to its normal length and position, and then join the broken ends. A poultice made of pulverized plant root was applied and the limb was held in place with wooden splints bound with cords. Just as doctors today insert metal pins to help hold mending bones together, so Aztec surgeons sometimes inserted sticks inside exposed bone fractures.

AZTEC DENTISTRY

The Aztecs took good care of their teeth, rinsing them with water after every meal and shifting food particles with thorns or

OPENING THE SKULL

The Inca performed successful surgery on people's skulls. In a technique we call trepanation they cut a hole in the skull, probably to relieve pressure on the brain caused by swelling as a result of blows to the head. The patient was given coca leaves to reduce the pain. We know that some survived this because trepanned skulls have been found showing evidence of healing.

toothpicks. Tartar was removed with charcoal in salted water, or with a mixture of salt, alum, chilli and cochineal applied using a root as a brush. Swollen and abscessed gums were pierced with thorns and cleaned of pus.

Although the Aztecs frequently drilled their teeth to decorate them with gold and precious stones, there is no evidence that they drilled them to remove decay.

MILITARY TECHNOLOGY

Fighting between rival peoples and city-states was a regular occurrence in Mesoamerica and the Andes. Men of both regions were encouraged to develop a fighting spirit. The Aztecs believed that human sacrifice kept the sun moving through the sky, so their warriors always looked for new victims to capture.

A life-size sculpture of an Aztec eagle warrior.

THE ARMY OF THE INCA

The Inca army was a large, well-disciplined force of men. Every male Inca was required to serve in the army at least once in his life. An Inca soldier's main weapons were a sling, a spear and a mace or club. The Inca, like the Aztecs, had no bronze or iron for making weapons. The Inca also recruited warriors from the tribes living in the tropical forests, as they were particularly skilled at using bows and arrows and shooting darts from blowpipes. At the start of a battle the soldiers attacked their opponents from a distance, first using slings and then their bows. When the two forces were close enough they fought hand to hand with clubs and spears. For protection, Inca soldiers carried shields made of wood or leather.

AZTEC WARRIORS

Aztec warriors were armed with wooden warclubs and spears that had sharp blades made of obsidian, a black glassy substance.

A spear from a weapon known as an *atlatl* (pronounced ot-lottle) could be hurled a long distance, further than 100 metres. The weapon had a wooden shaft with a handle on one end and a groove with a cup at the other end. The butt of the spear fitted into the cup. The spear was thrown by flicking the upper arm and wrist forwards. The Spanish discovered that a spear from an Aztec's *atlatl* pierced their armour.

Aztec warriors had shields made of wood or woven maize cane. Often, these were decorated with colourful feathers. They also wore close-fitting body armour made of quilted cotton that helped to soften the blow of an opponent's club. Successful warriors had helmets showing their membership of a warrior order. For example, the members of the Knights of the Eagle wore eagle-head helmets.

The thrower starts to throw an atlatl *like a javelin, then halfway through the action he flicks his arm and wrist forwards.*

THE SPANISH CONQUEST

Although greatly outnumbered by the armies of the Aztecs, Inca and other people, the Spanish conquistadors who arrived at the beginning of the 16th century won many victories because their technology was superior. They brought arquebuses (an early form of gun, mounted on a tripod), which shocked and amazed the natives. Aztec and Inca shields and armour of wood and cotton were no match for their steel swords, crossbows and pikestaffs. The horses and wardogs of the Spaniards were also used to terrifying effect.

41

Aztec, Inca and Maya timeline

c.3000 BC The first pottery is made in the Americas in what is now Colombia and Ecuador.

c.1150 BC The rise of the Olmec civilization in Mexico.

c.300 BC The beginning of the Mayan civilization in Mesoamerica. Large city-states are formed in Mexico, such as Teotihuacan.

AD **100** The decline of the Olmecs.

c.AD **500** The first great Mayan city of Tikal is founded.

c.AD **600** The Mayan civilization is at the height of its powers. An unknown event destroys the city of Teotihuacan.

c.AD **850** The collapse of the powerful Mayan culture.

AD **899** The city of Tikal is abandoned.

AD **1000** The Chimu culture appears in Peru.

c.AD **1100** The Toltecs build their capital at Tula in Mexico

c.AD **1200** The Aztecs move into the Valley of Mexico. Manco Cápac becomes the first Sapa Inca (emperor) and founds the Inca Empire.

AD **1325** The Aztec city of Tenochtitlan is founded. The Aztecs begin their rise to power in Mexico.

AD **1438** The Inca build the fortress of Sacsayhuaman and the city of Machu Picchu.

AD **1470** The Inca conquer the Chimu kingdom.

AD **1492** Christopher Columbus reaches the Americas, making landfall on the island of Hispaniola in the Antilles, and Europe discovers the New World.

AD **1493** The first Spanish settlement is established at Hispaniola. Portugal and Spain agree to divide the New World between them.

AD **1498** Columbus discovers the mainland of South America.

AD **1517** Spaniards under the command of Hernandez de Cordoba arrive in Yucatan (part of Mexico). They bring with them diseases such as smallpox, measles and influenza unknown in the New World. Within a century Mesoamerica's population will be devastated by these diseases.

AD **1519** Hernán Cortés begins the conquest of the Aztec empire.

AD **1521** Tenochtitlan is destroyed.

AD **1522** Tenochtitlan is rebuilt and renamed as Mexico City.

AD **1532** Francisco Pizarro begins the conquest of the Incan empire.

AD **1572** Tupac Amaru, the last Incan emperor, is captured and executed.

GLOSSARY

abrasive A hard-wearing substance used in grinding and polishing.

abscess A painful collection of pus that forms as a result of an infection.

acoustic Relating to sound and hearing.

adobe Sun-dried brick of mud and straw.

alloy A mixture of two or more metals. Bronze is an alloy of copper and tin.

alpaca A South American mammal, similar to a llama, that has silky soft wool.

balsa A boat of reed bundles tied together.

causeway A raised roadway for crossing marshy or swampy ground.

chapines (singular chapin) Blocks of dried mud for growing seedlings on a *chinampa*.

chasqui One of the trained runners who delivered messages along the Inca roads.

chinampa An Aztec system of reclaiming swampy land for planting crops.

chuño A freeze-dried potato product from the high plains of the Andes.

cochineal An insect that lives on cacti and which is fried and turned into a red dye.

codex A book written on parchment that is rolled up or folded.

embarro A mixture of red mud and weeds for building traditional Mayan houses.

embossing Decorating a piece of metal with a raised design.

glaze A hard, waterproof coat added to the surface of pottery.

glyph A picture or character that stands for a letter, a sound or a word.

gum A sticky substance from certain plants.

hieroglyph One of the picture symbols used in the Egyptian system of writing.

huaira An oven for smelting metals.

Huari A civilization that flourished in Peru between AD 600 and 1000.

ichu A tough grass from the Andes.

irrigation Supplying land with the water needed to ensure plant growth.

jerky A dried beef snack.

lapidary A craftsman who cuts and polishes precious stones.

masonry Stone or brick structures.

Mesoamerica A region that includes Mexico and Central America.

Mixtec An ancient civilization of skilled metalworkers from Mexico.

Moche A civilization that flourished in Peru between AD 100 and 800.

mortar A mixture of sand, cement and water for holding masonry blocks together.

obsidian A volcanic glass that can be turned into sharp-edged weapons and tools.

Olmec A great Mexican civilization that flourished from 1500 to 300 BC.

polygonal Having many sides.

poultice A moist plant pulp applied to wounds to reduce inflammation and aid healing.

pyramid A large building with a square base and four triangular sides rising to a point.

quilted Made of stitched layers of fabric.

quipu A series of knotted strings the Inca used for keeping records.

raising A technique for hammering a sheet of metal into a bowl.

sling A looped strap used to whirl and throw a small projectile such as a stone.

smelting Extracting metal from its ore by heating and melting.

splint A device for immobilizing and supporting a broken bone while it heals.

talud-tablero A style of architecture in which a platform (the *tablero*) rests on top of a sloping wall (the *talud*).

tamales A steamed maize parcel stuffed with meat or vegetable fillings.

tambo A resthouse on an Inca road where travellers found food and lodging.

Toltecs Warrior and trading people who lived in Mesoamerica from AD 900 to 1200.

Totonacs A people who lived in eastern Mexico at the time of the Spanish conquest.

tumbaga An alloy of copper and gold.

turquoise A blue-green, semi-precious stone that was highly prized by the Aztecs.

vicuña A South American mammal, similar to a llama, that is prized for its wool.

FURTHER READING

Step Into the Aztec and Maya Worlds by Fiona MacDonald (Southwater, 2007)
Hidden World of the Aztec by Peter Lourie (Boyd Mills Press, 2006)
Step Into the Inca World by Philip Steele (Southwater, 2006)
Aztec, Inca and Maya by Elizabeth Baquedano (Dorling Kindersley, 2005)
Arts and Crafts of the Aztecs and Maya by Ting Morris (Watts, 2006)

WEBSITES

http://www.indians.org/welker/aztec.htm
An introduction to the Aztecs, with links to many aspects of Aztec life.

http://www.wsu.edu/~dee/CIVAMRCA/AZTECS.HTM
An overview of Aztec civilization.

http://www.wsu.edu/~dee/CIVAMRCA/INCAS.HTM
An introduction to the Inca people.

http://www.42explore2.com/inca.htm
Links to explore various aspects of Inca life.

http://coe.fgcu.edu/students/webb/meso/maya.htm
A site exploring aspects of the Maya civilization.

INDEX